home STYLING
Contrasts in Design

MIKE
STROHL

PBC INTERNATIONAL, INC.

home STYLING
Contrasts in Design

Distributor to the book trade in the United States and Canada
Rizzoli International Publications Inc.
through St. Martin's Press
175 Fifth Avenue
New York, NY 10010

Distributor to the art trade in the United States and Canada
PBC International, Inc.
One School Street
Glen Cove, NY 11542

Distributor throughout the rest of the world
Hearst Books International
1350 Avenue of the Americas
New York, NY 10019

Library of Congress Cataloging-in-Publication Data
Strohl, Mike.
        Homestyling : contrasts in design / by Mike Strohl.
                    p.   cm.
        Includes index.
        ISBN 0-86636-684-9
        1.   Interior decoration.   I. Title
NK2110.S79   1998   98-51373
747—dc21   CIP

CAVEAT—Information in this text is believed accurate, and will pose no
problem for the student or casual reader. However, the author was often
constrained by information contained in signed release forms, information
that could have been in error or not included at all. Any misinformation
(or lack of information) is the result of failure in these attestations. The
author has done whatever is possible to insure accuracy.

10 9 8 7 6 5 4 3 2 1

TO KAREN FISHER FOR HER
EXAMPLE, INSPIRATION, AND SUPPORT.

contents

introduction

As we approach the millennium, the rate at which we exchange ideas is dazzling. An infinite range of design concepts from all over the world are available to us, and with no trends to speak of, our individual choices take on more significance than ever before. In spaces that reflect an undaunted freedom, furnishings may rotate, mirroring the adventurous nature of the people who inhabit them. Luxurious rooms are often created by using simple fabrics and found objects. A number of interior designers offer a decorating plan that the clients have largely developed for themselves. Some designers, like Clodagh, have gone so far as to study an apartment "so that it could look un-studied," and effectively highlight the clients' personalities. *Homestyling: Contrasts in Design* is a confident acceptance of informality, a fresh approach.

The eclecticism of this creative spirit has come into being, and it's all in the mix. *Homestyling: Contrasts in Design* represents a unique point in history in which traditional styles of the twenties and thirties, as all the decades following, have become elements of a rich palette — concepts that can be exchanged, borrowed, and placed side-by-side in a single room to form a beautiful pastiche. Thus, a sleek modernity can be achieved in an Art Deco-style building. A turn-of-the-century home can have an inherent sense of the realities of day-to-day living, and a new house can be infused with local folk art traditions. *Homestyling: Contrasts in Design* incorporates a respect for the past which is not restrictive. Nothing is so precious that it cannot be used, and with objects and furnishings that emphasize practicality, rooms display a vibrant rhythm of the contemporary and antique.

This heightened awareness of the many possibilities available in interior design is displayed in rooms that harbor myriad styles, varied traditions, and the notion that it's chic to be practical — like a prolific imagination, contrasts arise from a sense of spontaneity that is continually replenished with new discoveries.

Mike Strohl

away from it all

"I don't want to live in a theme park," states interior designer Celeste B. Cooper. For her own New York City apartment, Cooper sought to achieve a sense of tranquillity, simplicity, and calm, without turning to statement elements or period/style re-creations. She explains, "Design should be indigenous to the environment — I don't believe that adobe, for instance, is appropriate in New York."

The neutral, monochromatic colors of wall treatments, floors, fabrics, and furniture finishes contribute to the peaceful atmosphere and lend a sense of additional space to this urbane residence. Cooper is a great believer in the use of so-called naturals; beige, cream, and khaki "are always clean and timeless," she says. And the color palette, with sparingly positioned accents of bright colors, visually expands the space.

In the designer's opinion, when one is working in a tightly controlled space, the fewer the number of pieces employed the better. Cooper pared down the number of furnishings, making sure the scale was right. "You can't make any mistakes because you have no place to hide them," she says. With limited storage space, everything is "out," but the apartment is seamless. Cooper is an avid organizer, seeking out new storage solutions that, while functional, are also attractive.

Repertoire Interior Designer • **Richard Mandelkorn** Photographer
Metropolitan New York • 1,800 square feet/167 square meters

This New York City apartment is not only a place to live, but serves as a showcase and office for the designer. Flexibility is important in the small space, where rooms and furnishings must be multifunctional. The dining room is easily converted to an office in which to meet with clients.

The design concept is informed by function and feel. A textured wall evokes the natural environment, and a metal sculpture brings elemental purity to the urban locale. A work area is accented by ceramics and artifacts.

"The home is a refuge," says Cooper. Within the more private spaces of the apartment, there is a definite sense of retreat and escape from the cacophony of the urban jungle just outside. The natural palette assists in creating the mood.

room for living

"There are two focal points in the room: the fireplace and a view of the lake," explains interior designer Noel Jeffrey of the living room he composed for a renovated shingle-style showhouse in historic Southampton, New York. He divided the large room into two distinct seating areas — one around the hearth, the other oriented toward two walls of French doors that open onto a wraparound deck and lawn leading down to the shoreline.

"The challenge was to produce a luxurious room using simple fabrics and found objects, rather than rich fabrics and priceless antiques," he submits. "It's minimal and opulent at the same time." The palette selected has a fresh, seaside flavor, with the emphasis placed on white accented with clear blues and touches of complementary golden yellow tones. The clients desired a simple country look — not a clichéd baskets-and-wreaths style, but a crisp, jaunty, comfortable home.

19

Noel Jeffrey Inc. Interior Designer • **Peter Vitale** Photographer
Southampton, New York • 500 square feet/47 square meters

Instead of opting for a one-trick scheme, Jeffrey multiplied the function of the living room by two, creating two seating areas. A light and bright aesthetic was adopted — mostly painted furniture enhances the effect, with floors painted as well. Informal and genteel, the room is monochromatic, yet lively and inviting.

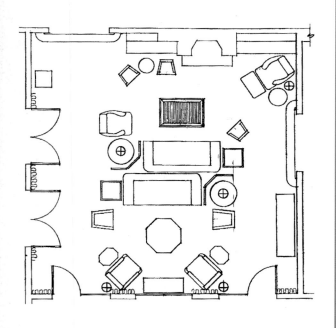

The space focused on the hearth is surrounded by an especially handsome set of customized shelves in which to display a range of collected objects. The clean line of architectural detail and the use of white provides a fresh, summery mood.

practical luxury

"The best luxuries are ultimately practical." So states architect/designer William Sofield, who resides in a 1929 apartment house. Shared with two dalmatians, the apartment offers an elegant character with an inherent sense of the realities of day-to-day living.

Natural materials figure prominently in the decorative scheme, creating warmth and luxe. Cashmere, wool, aged leather, polished rosewood, ebonized oak, parchment, and raffia are among the materials that were brought together not only for their handsomeness when used in concert, but for practicality's sake. For instance, raffia is used as a wainscoting in the bedroom, protecting the walls where they are most vulnerable. All the fabrics — such as the leather upholstery on the club chairs and a wool frisé on the sofa — can withstand the roughest treatment. Sumptuous cashmere curtains in the sitting room may seem extravagant, yet the material prevents heat loss in the winter months, blocks the sun's rays in summer, assists in keeping the apartment cooler, and muffles the ever-present city hum.

Sofield's take on comfort? "If it's not comfortable, what's the point?" That goes not only for the furniture, as there is a kind of comfort associated with surrounding yourself with objects you love. Says Sofield, "I don't acquire furniture or objects that are so fragile, precious, or bizarre that they can't be used."

Studio Sofield Interior Designer • **Laura Resen** Photographer
Metropolitan New York • 1,500 square feet/139 square meters

Furniture pieces of many periods and styles, chosen for their functionality, are juxtaposed in a pleasing fashion throughout the apartment. A large and interesting variety of objects, collected over the years and periodically rearranged, abound in every room.

golden moment

A spacious house situated on an idyllic stretch of land with mature plantings along the water would seem to be a dream-come-true type of design project. It was for the owner of this estate, who worked closely with architect Peter Bernholz to create a highly personal, always summery, intuitive kind of home. "The house was originally a reproduction of a Mediterranean villa, circa 1900, and was reborn as a statement of the owner's love of antiques, water, gardens, and objects, " says Bernholz.

The structure possesses the flavor of a turn-of-the-century mansion. A respect for the past remains, but it is not a consuming or restrictive one. Two upstairs bedrooms were sacrificed, for example, to create a dramatic vertical center hall. Yet, opulent details, and the elegant flow from room to room were preserved as evidence of the house's rich history.

The mix of fabrics includes cotton, silk, damask, lace, and velvet. Antiques from the owner's large and well-selected collection, which were in previous residences, are integrated into the house, mixed with flea market finds, architectural objects, and Art Nouveau accessories. A country house mood permeates the spaces, where softness rules and a romantic concept of living is embraced.

31

Bernholz Associates Architects Architect • **Alex McLean** Photographer
Metropolitan New York • 7,000 square feet/650 square meters

Rooms in this renovated estate are casually arranged with conversation areas. No stiffness is allowed, and the idea of strict formality was dismissed. Everything is closely edited, so that the mélange of elements exudes a feeling of faded gentility.

While the house was completely renovated, many elements of the original Mediterranean villa were retained, emphasized, or improved upon, especially in terms of the new tiled double-height entry hall and original leaded-glass windows. A vast collection of objects, which display a wide taste of styles and forms, is interspersed throughout every room of the house.

A relaxed environment with spaces one associates with English country houses is present in the home. French doors and extensive glazing were introduced to give full visual, as well as physical access to the tremendous grounds surrounding the house. The relationship between interior and exterior spaces is open and friendly.

Bedrooms present a soft, drapey, feminine mien. Antique dresses are creatively displayed as textural, colorful artwork. The color palette throughout the house is muted, but varied.

refined movement

A strong color and materials palette, when used in a consistent way, breeds a certain simplicity. This family residence represents the successful synthesis of a fascinating collection of strongly architectural furnishings and stylistically diverse works of art from a number of periods.

Brought together by interior designer Barbara Hauben-Ross, the confluence is tamed, and what seemingly should not work does in a way that is remarkable and extremely striking. Contemporary is meshed with antique; colors blend to make a strong impression that is harmonious to the eye.

Linking the whole are several specifically selected or designed components. Cherry architectural moldings and paneling, for instance, are seen in several rooms, including the sleek bathrooms. Such details outline or highlight the spaces as a visual constant which relates to the finish of the furniture. Hauben-Ross has given the apartment a grammar all its own, and the punctuation is perfect.

42

Barbara Hauben-Ross, Inc. Interior Designer • **Michael LeClere** Architect • **Billy Cunningham** Photographer
Metropolitan New York • 8,000 square feet/743 square meters

Hauben-Ross designed the carpet in the living room especially for the project. The library/media room upstairs gets a different treatment in terms of color, as befits a contemporary-era invention. The design is "respectful of historic precedent, yet updated and catholic in its taste," says Hauben-Ross.

New custom elements are matched with the interesting array of pieces on display in the two-level apartment. Fabrics employed throughout are either plains or wovens, for a look that is in keeping with the mostly early-to-mid-twentieth century furnishings the owners have collected.

*Elements executed in American cherry — "the traditional wood used during the Arts and Crafts period,"
lend warmth and an organic quality to several spaces within the apartment, says Hauben-Ross.*

rural reflection

Interior designer Mary Douglas Drysdale spends weekends away from her busy firms in Washington, D.C. and New York City at a renovated farmhouse in rural Pennsylvania. The eighteenth-century stone house required complete gutting, restoration, and decoration, but creating newness out of old was not Drysdale's intent. Finishes and furnishings have the patina and eclectic feel of a home that has evolved out of the local folk traditions.

The relatively small rooms of the 1,200-square-foot house were opened up, literally by knocking down walls, and atmospherically by means of adding larger window openings that admit more natural light. In most rooms, there are no window treatments. If so, a simple swag or shade sets off the views of the surrounding landscape and is also available when privacy is desired.

Floors are wide wood planking, some only bleached and sanded, while others are stained, painted, and stenciled in a way that gives a nod to Amish practices. Rough-hewn original beams throughout the three-level residence are left exposed, providing an interesting contrast to the smooth, clean surfaces of furnishings. In the public rooms of the house, spareness reigns, though it is achieved using pieces that reflect the period in which the house was built. Upstairs, bright colors enter the fray with pleasing results, reflecting the "not-always-safe" Drysdale approach to design.

Drysdale Design Associates Interior Designer • **Andrew Lautman** Photographer
Eastern Pennsylvania • 3,000 square feet / 279 square meters

The house's original kitchen and living room were joined to make a larger, more open living and dining space. A new kitchen was added with architectural elements reminiscent of those original to the house. In the dressing area of the master bedroom, Drysdale installed a deep copper soaking tub.

Color invigorates the third-floor combination guest room/den. An alcove was created by enclosing a space under the eaves, which holds a curtained bed. Softer tones were applied to the sleeping portion of the master bedroom, in which walls are stenciled and original interior shutters are found on the windows.

familiar territory

"All the antiques have been used and re-used, some for over 35 years, in different rooms and homes, and the sofas and chairs have been reupholstered many times," says John Eric Sebesta regarding the decoration of this light and airy Central Park West residence. The finely tuned rooms created by Sebesta and partner Betty Lou Baker incorporate sleek ultra-contemporary pieces with English, French, Scandinavian, and German period pieces from the eighteenth through the twentieth century.

Simple window treatments are carefully fashioned to integrate varied light levels, and few fabric patterns are introduced. Prominence is given to the interesting array of objects, including expensive and inexpensive artifacts from Africa, America, and Russia. The mix reflects the owner's exposure to the multitude of cultures and design ideas present in New York City. What these objects all share, explains Sebesta, is a sense of integrity and a continuity of taste — "Spare but not cold, simple but sophisticated, refined but not effete."

59

Baker & Sebesta Interiors Interior Designer • **Kari Haavisto** Photographer
Metropolitan New York • 3,500 square feet/325 square meters

A minimal amount of color allows each element within the apartment to be seen clearly. Simple valenced curtains allow for an abundance of natural light to enter the spaces and clear views out to Central Park. With few patterns introduced, the overall effect is soothing.

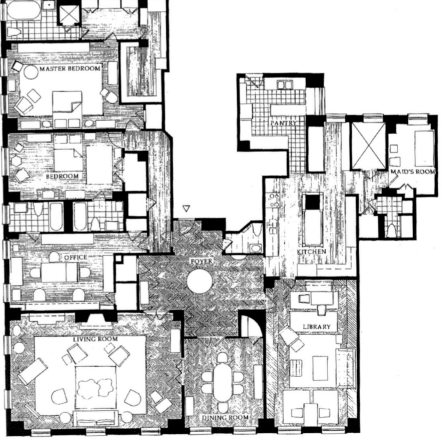

"Comfort was our top priority," says designer John Eric Sebesta, of the apartment he and Betty Lou Baker composed, re-using and incorporating many items collected over the years.

at ease

"Every inch counts," says interior designer Tom Fox, describing his own apartment in a renovated brownstone. "Every object is to be used and must serve a purpose." Fox composed a pleasing array of stylish, yet practical furnishings, mixing contemporary and antique without going overboard with frills or cramming too much in. "It all creates a rhythm," he states.

The designer avoided a heavy treatment, which can "lock itself into a period." Fox created a home in which objects can be moved as the mood strikes him and as he continues to amass items for his collections. This concept extends to the background color of the walls. "Fixed, calculated color schemes irritate my senses," he explains. "I wanted a clean, white space for color to pass through." A minimal backdrop allows for interiors which change with the designer's discoveries and tastes. This flexible, evolving design scheme is given primary importance in the home of Fox, who believes that decorating is an ongoing process.

Fox-Nahem Interior Designer • **Pieter Estersohn** Photographer
Metropolitan New York • 700 square feet/65 square meters

Because of space constraints, a relaxed sense of order is evident in every room. Yet while there are places and purposes for everything introduced into the space, one is never left with an impression of the rooms as stage sets.

mission control

Though it's a sprawling, 9,000-square-foot oceanfront house, a cozy sensibility is communicated throughout the rooms of this beach cottage residence of comedy club owner, Caroline Hirsch. "While the dramatic entry hall is double height, the moment you move into the adjacent spaces a mellow intimacy prevails," says interior designer Glenn Gissler.

While the scale of the rooms is generous with many open views, the spaces are divided into smaller seating areas where comfort is the rule. There is plenty of breathing room and certainly no overcrowding. Curtains, when they do appear, are quite simple. In many cases, windows are undressed, allowing for spectacular views of the ocean and dunes up and down the shore.

The shingle-style roots of the house are respected, but the design is not limited to a single period style. Eighteenth, nineteenth, and early twentieth-century antiques mingle with custom upholstered furniture, a wide variety of lamps, and ceiling fixtures. If a theme can be identified, it is the deployment of the large collection of original American Mission and English Arts and Crafts furnishings that can be found in the mix. These handcrafted, architecturally simple pieces anchor the overall scheme, and harmonize well — even with the most contemporary of Gissler's choices.

70

Glenn Gissler Design, Inc. Interior Designer • **Francis Fleetwood** Architect • **Andrew Bordwin** Photographer
Metropolitan New York • 9,000 square feet/836 square meters

Dark-stained wide plank oak floors were installed throughout the cottage. A strategy for color was determined at the outset of the project, with cream established as the brightest "white" to be used. Wall colors maximize the impact of the seaside light.

A subtle richness pervades the house. Plain fabrics, stripes, and a few small-scale patterns serve as a counterpoint to the bolder patterns found in numerous turn-of-the-century Persian rugs installed in various rooms. Painted bead board paneling is used in bathrooms to add texture and warmth to surfaces.

classical comfort

"Classic concepts in a personal point of view," is how designer Andrew Frank defines his own Park Avenue apartment. Rather than depicting a specific period style when creating his home, Frank desired a flexible, yet intriguing space that would serve for both private time and entertaining clients. A clean, classically modern design fit the designer's idea, and encompassed the accents of his individual style.

Subtle, muted shades play a major role in the color scheme. Neutrals allow the shapes of furnishings to be accentuated — a sleigh bed, for example, is given prominence in the bedroom. Natural colors also enhance the rich architectural surroundings; eleven-foot-high ceilings, double foyer, and fireplace lend a sense of grandeur to the apartment, while beams, herringbone oak floors, and cove moldings characterize the prewar structure.

Elements of Art Deco style are evident, such as in a tassled light fixture in the bedroom. Yet Frank finishes all his projects with accessories which have come to embody a certain signature. They often refer to architectural fragments, black-and-white photos, and clean shapes that, as Frank states, "remain timeless in their design and conception."

79

Andrew Frank Interior Design Interior Designer • **Peter Margonelli** Photographer
Metropolitan New York • 1,100 square feet/102 square meters

"It means waking up in the morning and still enjoying your environment," states Frank about a design which transcends trends. In his own apartment, furnishings are accentuated — the unusual placement of a sleigh bed against a window enhances the largess of the bedroom. Neutral colors provide a calm, soothing background for the rich architectural play of cove moldings, beams, and herringbone oak floors.

cultured pearl

The owners of this New York City apartment in a historic prewar building on Central Park West amassed an impressive and very fine array of furniture, works of art, and decorative objects from around the world, including a museum quality pottery collection. Interior designers Carl D'Aquino and Geordi Humphreys were especially sensitive about creating an environment that reflects and enhances the owners' aesthetic choices. "This home glows with rose, magenta, ochre, gold, bronze, and iron," explain the designers, noting that the selected color scheme is based on the hues seen within the ceramic collection.

American art pottery is displayed in custom designed, lighted cabinetwork in the library. Yet the formal presentation is counterbalanced by the owners' "adventurous nature" explains D'Aquino, who relates that the display is not static: "the clients are not afraid to rotate and move pieces throughout the apartment."

While luxurious in appearance, the apartment is inherently practical. Antique furnishings were deliberately selected for size and ease of use, and the unique art pottery floors are easy to maintain. As D'Aquino states, "this is a home to be lived in."

Carl D'Aquino Interiors Inc. Interior Designer • **John Hall/Guy Lindsay** Photographers
Metropolitan, New York • 1,800 square feet/167 square meters

A multitude of patterns and textures are combined throughout the apartment. It's all in the mix. "No one is going to swoon when they enter a room and notice that you've matched your 'barely beige' travertine to a 'basically bone' Berber," says D'Aquino.

While the touchstone for the interior design was the owners' extensive collection of pottery, the Craftsman-era apartment building in which they reside also influenced D'Aquino's aesthetic choices.

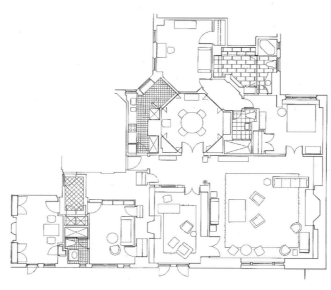

superb remake

The dilemma: a fairly mundane 1950s ranch-style house in suburban Westchester County, New York, with generously sized, but boxy rooms. The desire: a sophisticated, somewhat glamorous environment suitable for frequent entertaining with a centrally located family room. The solution: a more open plan, a soft color palette, attention to detail, and touches of luxury.

Interior designer Joan Halperin advised her clients to go simple, but sumptuous. She linked all the public rooms by designing more gracious double-door openings. "By aligning these openings, the spaces progress one after another, creating interior vistas and a generous flow appropriate for parties," she explains.

The color scheme of the interior incorporates creams, ivory, and off-whites, with punctuations of subtle pale gold, rich deep blue, and dark wood tones. Texture is favored over pattern.

By choosing fewer pieces of furniture, mindful always of form and scale, the impact of each counts for more. "Period and provenance have been ignored," says Halperin, "but everything is understated." Some things were purchased new; others, such as the Stickley-style sofa, were reworked into cleaner, simpler, and more elegant pieces that contribute to the calm, scrupulously edited, and rather timeless contemporary setting.

91

Joan Halperin/Interior Design Interior Designer • **Adrianne dePolo** Photographer
Harrison, New York • 3,500 square feet/325 square meters

A faint Art Deco taste is discernible, though this is certainly not an exercise in re-creating an era. After frequent trips to Paris, the clients became fond of the style, which is reflected by the scheme's pervading curvilinear geometry.

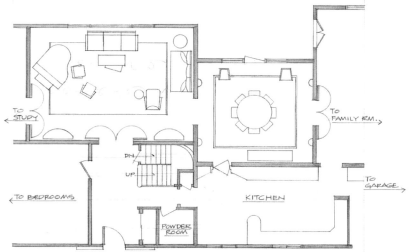

art & industry

When does an interior become a home? In interior designer Clodagh's mind, a home is created by the introduction of natural materials, rich velvets, heathery paisleys, subtle lighting, and the ability to focus on the inhabitant's personal preferences.

Used as a residence and office, this apartment is, in Clodagh's opinion, "not a decorator house." She adds, "It will never look like a designer just left. The people living here have the confidence to allow the designer to highlight *them*, their possessions, and their collections."

To achieve this, Clodagh "studied everything so that it could look un-studied." Simple window and wall treatments are downplayed to allow furnishings, artwork, and personal objects to take center stage. The walls and ceilings are sponge-treated, providing a muted, less defined geometry within the spaces. The overall palette is warm. In the living room, an enormous hearth composed of demolition brick was built, bringing additional texture and a country feeling to the apartment.

Clodagh Design International Interior Designer/Architect • **Daniel Aubry** Photographer
Metropolitan New York • 1,750 square feet/163 square meters

This apartment designed by Clodagh is artfully crafted. Collected pieces, which include furnishings and objects of an unusual nature, are displayed against subtly textured walls. Many of the rooms play double, even triple, roles. The entry hall, for example, is used as a dining room, and is also set up as a gallery space.

The rustic feeling of the hearth extends throughout the apartment. A four-poster bed and antique trunk take center stage in the bedroom, where kilims and soft colors provide a soothing background.

directory

ARCHITECTS AND INTERIOR DESIGNERS

ANDREW FRANK INTERIOR DESIGN
Andrew Frank
530 Park Avenue
New York, New York 10021
Tel: (212) 832-3205
Fax: (212) 750-8084

BAKER & SEBESTA INTERIORS
Betty Lou Baker
John Eric Sebesta
146 Central Park West
New York, New York 10023
Tel: (212) 787-3236
Fax: (212) 787-2427

BARBARA HAUBEN-ROSS, INC.
Barbara Hauben-Ross
226 East 54th Street
New York, New York 10022
Tel: (212) 832-6640
Fax: (212) 421-3358

BERNHOLZ ASSOCIATES ARCHITECTS
Peter M. Bernholz, AIA
306 East 61st Street
New York, New York 10021
Tel: (212) 838-6743
Fax: (212) 755-3987

CARL D'AQUINO INTERIORS, INC.
Carl D'Aquino
Geordi Humphreys
180 Varick Street
New York, New York 10014
Tel: (212) 929-9787
Fax: (212) 929-9225

CLODAGH DESIGN INTERNATIONAL
Clodagh
Ray Booth
Robert Pierpoint
365 First Avenue
New York, New York 10010
Tel: (212) 673-9202
Fax: (212) 614-9125

DRYSDALE DESIGN ASSOCIATES
Mary Douglas Drysdale
1733 Connecticut Avenue NW
Washington, D.C. 20008
Tel: (202) 588-0700
Fax: (202) 588-5086

FRANCIS FLEETWOOD, AIA
25 Newtown Lane
East Hampton, New York 11937
Tel: (516) 324-4994
Fax: (516) 324-0057

FOX-NAHEM DESIGN
Thomas Fox
69 Fifth Avenue
New York, New York 10003
Tel: (212) 929-1485
Fax: (212) 645-3136

GLENN GISSLER DESIGN, INC.
Glenn Gissler
174 Fifth Avenue
New York, New York 10010
Tel: (212) 727-3220
Fax: (212) 727-3225

JOAN HALPERIN/INTERIOR DESIGN
Joan Halperin
401 East 80th Street
New York, New York 10021
Tel: (212) 288-8636
Fax: (212) 472-3743

MICHAEL LeCLERE
16 East 52nd Street
New York, New York 10022
Tel: (212) 328-6550
Fax: (212) 368-2744

NOEL JEFFREY, INC.
Noel Jeffrey
215 East 58th Street
New York, New York 10021
Tel: (212) 935-7775
Fax: (212) 935-8280

REPERTOIRE
Celeste B. Cooper, ASID
325 East 57th Street
New York, New York 10022
Tel: (212) 826-5667
Fax: (212) 935-7926

STUDIO SOFIELD
William Sofield
380 Lafayette Street
New York, New York 10003
Tel: (212) 473-1300
Fax: (212) 473-0300

PHOTOGRAPHERS

ANDREW BORDWIN
70A Greenwich Avenue
New York, New York 10011
Tel: (212) 285-2158
Fax: (212) 633-1046

BILLY CUNNINGHAM
140 Seventh Avenue
New York, New York 10011
Tel: (212) 929-6313

ADRIANNE dePOLO
18 ½ McKinley Street
Rowayton, Connecticut 06853
Tel: (203) 838-3583
Fax: (203) 831-0349

DANIEL AUBRY STUDIOS
Daniel Aubry
365 First Avenue
New York, New York 10010
Tel: (212) 598-4190
Fax: (212) 505-7670

PIETER ESTERSOHN
420 East 54th Street
New York, New York 10022
Tel: (212) 838-3170
Fax: (212) 758-6199

KARI HAAVISTO
25 West 15th Street
New York, New York 10011
Tel: (212) 807-6760
Fax: (212) 675-2502

JOHN HALL
885 Tenth Avenue
New York, New York 10019
Tel: (212) 957-0369
Fax: (212) 956-1462

LAUTMAN PHOTOGRAPHY
Andrew Lautman
4906 41st Street NW
Washington, D.C. 20016
Tel: (202) 966-2800
Fax: (202) 966-4240

GUY LINDSAY
180 Varick Street
New York, New York 10014
Tel/Fax: (212) 929-9787

RICHARD MANDELKORN
65 Beaver Pond Road
Lincoln, Massachusetts 01773
Tel: (617) 259-3310
Fax: (617) 259-3312

PETER MARGONELLI
20 Desbrosses Street
New York, New York 10013
Tel: (212) 941-0380
Fax: (212) 334-4449

ALEX McLEAN
158 Flushing Avenue
Brooklyn, New York 11205
Tel/Fax: (718) 875-9240

PETER VITALE PHOTOGRAPHY
Peter Vitale
P.O. Box 10126
Santa Fe, New Mexico 87504
Tel: (505) 988-2558

LAURA RESEN
29 Bethune Street
New York, New York 10014
Tel: (212) 620-3153
Fax: (212) 627-0647

index

acknowledgments

My thanks to the staff of
PBC International, Inc., the interior designers,
architects and photographers whose work
appears in these pages, and to all those whose
efforts contributed to the completion of
Homestyling: Contrasts in Design.